Herefordshire & Worcestershire's Los

by
Peter Dale

The first station at Stourbridge Junction, closed in 1901.

**The publishers regret that they cannot supply
copies of any pictures featured in this book.**

ACKNOWLEDGEMENTS

The publishers wish to thank the following for contributing photographs to this book:
John Alsop for the front cover, the inside front cover and pages 1, 4, 6–12, 18–21, 24, 26,
30, 31, 33–35, 39, 41, 42, 44, 46 and 47; and R.C. Casserley for pages 2, 3, 5, 13–17, 22, 23,
25, 27–29, 32, 36–38, 40, 43, 45, 48, the inside back cover and the back cover.

Moorhampton Station, looking towards Brecon, 23 April 1958.

INTRODUCTION

Herefordshire and Worcestershire are two counties combined for administration purposes and so it makes sense to combine them for this book. They cover an area of great diversity: the north of Worcestershire penetrates the industrial areas of the Black Country and Birmingham while west Herefordshire has the beautiful country of the Welsh borders. In railway terms the two counties were dominated by the Great Western Railway, the largest pre-Grouping company in terms of route mileage, but significant other companies were the London & North Western Railway and the Midland Railway, the second and fourth largest pre-Grouping companies respectively. Oddly the LNWR only had a short section of its own line, just 2.1 miles between Red Hill Junction on the Hereford to Abergavenny line and Rotherwas Junction on the Hereford to Gloucester line. It exercised running powers over the GWR to reach the Abergavenny to Merthyr line and owned the Shrewsbury & Hereford Railway jointly with the GWR.

Railways came early to the area: the Hay Railway opened in 1816, although this line did not carry passengers and was horse-worked. The first public railway in the two counties was the section of the London & Birmingham Railway which crossed the north-east of Worcestershire and opened in April 1838.

In the far west of the area there were some fascinating, bucolic rural lines which have all gone. In retrospect, it might be thought obvious that these areas could never support a railway, yet they were promoted with high hopes. Justifiably so, as the Kington & Eardisley line replaced the horse-worked Kington Railway which had yielded dividends as high as 3½ per cent just hauling goods. But circumstances had changed: in earlier times the area had looked to South Wales for its links as the natural line of transport by the river and canal led that way. By the 1860s Kington was linked by rail with the rest of Herefordshire and on to London and the line from Eardisley to Swansea saw only two through passenger trains a day. Goods and services flowed in a different direction but the promoters of the K&ER had not realised that.

It is worth adding a word of explanation here about the Grouping for non-railway enthusiasts. Many of the railways in Britain were built by small companies, sometimes with the backing of a larger company. In the years leading up to 1923 there was a process of consolidation by which smaller companies amalgamated or were absorbed by larger ones, but in 1922 there were still well over 100 different companies in Britain. In 1923 all but a few minor companies were grouped into four larger concerns by Act of Parliament. These were the Great Western Railway (which continued in an enlarged form), the Southern Railway, the London, Midland & Scottish Railway (LMS – which included the LNWR and Midland) and the London & North Eastern Railway (LNER). These four companies – often referred to as the 'Big Four' – continued until nationalisation in 1948.

Under British Railways a Modernisation Plan introduced in 1955 spelled the beginning of the end for steam on Britain's railways, while the Beeching Plan of 1963 saw the start of widespread closures of many minor, and some major, lines.

Stourbridge has a special place in railway history as the early locomotive builder Foster Rastrick & Co. was based there. Their best known locos are the 'Agenoria', built for a local line, and the 'Stourbridge Lion', which was one of the first locomotives in the USA. Both still survive.

It is hoped this book will evoke memories for older readers of the relaxed form of travelling before the advent of motorways and perhaps encourage younger ones to make the acquaintance of the preserved lines in the area – The Severn Valley Railway at Kidderminster and the Gloucester–Warwickshire Railway at Toddington.

Weston-under-Penyard Halt, looking towards Hereford, 13 May 1961.

Birmingham & Gloucester Loop *

Passenger service withdrawn	17 June 1963	*Stations closed*	*Date*
Distance	28.0 miles (Redditch to Ashchurch)	Bengeworth	8 June 1953
Company	Midland Railway	Evesham	17 June 1963
		Harvington	1 October 1962
		Redditch **	4 May 1868
		Redditch ***	7 February 1973

A 'Strawberry Special' leaving Evesham Station.

* Closed stations on this line that were in Gloucestershire were Beckford, Ashton-under-Hill and Hinton. Those in Warwickshire were Salford Priors, Broom, Wixford, Alcester, Coughton and Studley & Astwood Bank.

** The first station closed when the line was extended to Alcester and a new station opened about 500 yards to the south.
*** This was replaced by the present station in 1973.

Harvington Station, looking south, *c.*1912.

The Birmingham & Gloucester Loop ran from the Midland Railway at Ashchurch to Birmingham via Evesham and Redditch. The oldest part of the line from Barnt Green to Redditch, opened in September 1859 and built by the Redditch Railway, is the only part still open. The southern section, the Evesham branch of the Midland, from Ashchurch, opened on 1 October 1864. The connecting link was the Evesham & Redditch Railway. This came about when the people of Evesham felt they needed better links with the north. It was authorised in July 1863 and opened from Evesham to Alcester on 17 September 1866 and to Redditch on 4 May 1868. Services were worked by the Midland, which absorbed the Redditch Railway in 1865 and the Evesham & Redditch in 1882.

Redditch Station.

Through trains were worked from Birmingham New Street to and from Ashchurch, with a number of shorter workings to and from Evesham from each end of the line. The line provided a useful alternative to the Midland main line and its challenging climb up the Lickey. It also provided links with the GWR at Evesham and the Stratford-upon-Avon & Midland Junction Railway at Broom. In its earlier days, the line carried large quantities of market garden produce from Evesham. Such crops are seasonal but traffic began in March with early vegetables and carried on until Christmas. Cabbages, Brussels sprouts, onions, asparagus, peas, strawberries, damsons, tomatoes, marrows, apples and pears were sent, but greatest of them all was the amount of plums sent by train. In August and September the Midland was sending about 1,000 tons of plums per week. The Midland sent six trains of garden produce away each day (and don't forget the GWR was carrying its share of the traffic as well) and trains were sent to the west (Gloucester), the north (Birmingham), and London, before re-marshalling to end up in such diverse places as Barnstaple or Manchester.

Gloucester to Ledbury *

Passenger service withdrawn	13 July 1959	*Stations closed*	*Date*
Distance	17.2 miles	Ledbury Town Halt	13 July 1959
Company	Newent Railway/Ross & Ledbury Railway		

* The closed stations on this line that were Gloucestershire were Barbers Bridge, Malswick Halt, Newent, Four Oaks Halt, Dymock and Greenway Halt.

The first scheme to bring modern transportation to the area between Ledbury and Gloucester was the Herefordshire & Gloucestershire Canal. Although it opened from the River Severn to Ledbury in 1798, it was not opened throughout until 1845. By this time canals were experiencing severe competition from railways and the canal directors, far-sightedly, saw the prospect of using the route of the canal as a railway. Consequently, before the opening through to Hereford, they started to look for a railway company as a prospective purchaser. There were a number of proposals, but it was 1873 before two schemes presented bills to Parliament. One of these schemes failed, having been opposed by the Severn Commissioners on the basis that a bridge would not have been high enough to allow ships to pass beneath. The successful scheme was proposed by the Newent Railway and the Ross & Ledbury Railway, which proposed a line as far as Ross but got no further than a junction with the Newent Railway. Difficulties were experienced raising the required capital and it was not until the GWR stepped in that progress was made. The canal closed at the end of June 1881 and the line opened throughout on 27 July 1885. It was worked by the GWR, which took over the local companies on 1 July 1892. The section from Dymock to Ledbury was made double track in case the line to Ross was proceeded with. Through goods trains were worked over the line for many years as it was shorter than the earlier GWR route from Gloucester to Birmingham via Hereford. In 1907 the North Warwickshire line opened and all but one of these were diverted via Honeybourne. The only station in Herefordshire did not open until 26 November 1928; it was more convenient for the town than the junction station. Latterly the line was worked by GWR diesel railcars.

Golden Valley Railway

Abbeydore Station.

Passenger service withdrawn	20 April 1898 (Pontrilas to Dorstone); 15 December 1941 (the final closure date after reopening by the GWR in May 1901)
Distance	18.7 miles (Pontrilas to Hay Junction)
Company	Golden Valley Railway

Stations closed	*Date*
Abbeydore	15 December 1941
Bacton *	15 December 1941
Vowchurch	15 December 1941
Peterchurch	15 December 1941
Dorstone	15 December 1941
Westbrook	15 December 1941
Greens Siding	15 December 1941
Clifford	15 December 1941

* This station was known as Bacton Road until 1 July 1903.

Vowchurch Station.

The Golden Valley Railway obtained its Act on 13 July 1876 and opened to Dorstone on 1 September 1881. The promoters were, as usual, over-optimistic and the extension from Dorstone to Hay was seen as part of an important link between Liverpool and Bristol. It was authorised on 7 August 1884 and opened on 27 May 1889. Despite several attempts to persuade the GWR to work the line, the terms offered by the directors were unacceptable to the GWR. The line was beset with financial difficulties and there were short periods when the line closed. The first of these was from 22 October to 16 November 1883 when the GWR withdrew the loco it had hired to the company due to non-payment of rent! It closed again between 2 July and 19 August 1885, ostensibly for re-sleepering but the real reason may have been to replace a GWR train with one of the company's. The Dorstone to Hay section was given up on 23 August 1897 due to the track being unsafe and the company finally gave up on 20 April 1898 when the Pontrilas to Dorstone section closed. The line was then bought by the GWR which reopened it throughout on 1 May 1901. The passenger service closed as an economy measure during the Second World War, although goods traffic survived until the 1950s. There was a large Ministry of Supply depot, opened in 1941, branching off the line just north of Pontrilas.

Peterchurch Station.

The GWR provided a service of three return trains daily with an extra one as far as Dorstone on Wednesday mornings. In 1901 a passenger could leave Dorstone on a Wednesday at 7.55 a.m. and be in Paddington at 2.20 p.m. although the rest of the week he or she could lie in and catch the 10.52 a.m., arriving at Paddington at 4.10 p.m. In 1922 there were two daily return trains with an additional one as far as Dorstone. Through trains took a little more than an hour and most ran as mixed trains.

Dorstone Station, *c*.1930.

The service was at first worked by a loco hired from the GWR but in 1883 the company obtained a 'Crewe Goods' loco converted into a tank loco. Two further similar locos followed in 1890 and 1892. The line's first coaches came from the Oldbury company but in 1885 they were returned to the builder because of financial difficulties and two coaches were bought from the Bishop's Castle Railway, which was in liquidation. In 1893 the debenture holders had to buy two four-wheelers from the London & South Western Railway to maintain the service after a contractor impounded the rolling stock for non-payment of rent.

Westbrook Station, 13 August 1932.

Clifford Station.

GWR to Bewdley

Passenger service withdrawn	5 January 1970	*Stations closed*	*Date*
Distance	3 miles	Foley Park *	5 January 1970
	(Kidderminster Junction to Bewdley)	Rifle Range Halt	closed sometime after 1930.
Company	Great Western Railway		

* This station was known as Foley Park Halt until 6 May 1968.

This line was built by the GWR and opened on 1 June 1878. Trains for the Tenbury line travelled over it and there was an intensive service of railmotors between Kidderminster and Bewdley. In 1910 there were fourteen up (i.e. towards Bewdley) and eleven down trains, most of which served Stourport as well. There were two return Sunday trains. By 1922 the service had grown to no less than 24 daily up trains between Kidderminster and Bewdley and 20 down trains. After the line closed it was taken over as part of the preserved Severn Valley Railway, giving that line a link into Kidderminster.

Halesowen Railway *

Passenger service withdrawn	April 1919	*Stations closed*	*Date*
Distance	5.9 miles (Halesowen to Northfield Junction)	Longbridge	by 1922
Company	Halesowen Railway	Rubery **	6 January 1964
		Hunnington **	1 September 1958

Locomotive No. 7432 at Longbridge Station, 8 April 1957.

The Halesowen Railway had its origins in a scheme of 1865 to link Halesowen with Bromsgrove but it didn't actually open until 18 years later and never reached the latter town. The Halesowen & Bromsgrove Railway was proposed after both the Birmingham & Gloucester and the Stourbridge railways by-passed Halesowen. A further scheme was promoted by the West Midland Railway to link Halesowen with the Stourbridge line at Old Hill. The Halesowen & Bromsgrove Branch Railway was formed in July 1865 but did not open until 10 September 1883, by which time it had changed its name to the Halesowen Railway and dropped its plans for a line to Bromsgrove, concentrating solely on what had been planned initially as a branch to Longbridge. It was worked by the Midland and GWR and became jointly owned by those companies in July 1906. After the Grouping it continued as a joint LMS/GWR line. The service in 1910 consisted of five trains in each direction on weekdays only. The most important source of traffic was the Austin factory at Longbridge, which opened in 1915 (the branch platform for it opened in February that year). Workmen's trains continued long after the public service was withdrawn, to Old Hill until September 1958 and to Northfields until 1964.

* The closed station on this line that was in Shropshire was Halesowen. A station is shown at Frankley on a map of 1904, but it does not appear in the timetable and no closure date is available for it.

** These stations remained open for workmen after the public service was withdrawn.

Hereford, Hay & Brecon Railway *

Passenger service withdrawn	31 December 1962		*Stations closed*	*Date*
Distance	25.6 miles (Brecon Curve Junction, Hereford,		Westmoor **	31 December 1962
	to Three Cocks Junction)		Moorhampton	31 December 1962
Company	Hereford, Hay & Brecon Railway		Kinnersley	31 December 1962
			Eardisley	31 December 1962
Stations closed	*Date*		Whitney-on-Wye ***	31 December 1962
Hereford Moorfields	1 April 1874		Hay-on-Wye ****	31 December 1962
Credenhill	31 December 1962			

Credenhill Station.

* The closed station on this line that was in Brecknockshire was Glasbury-on-Wye.

** This was a private station, sometimes known as Westmoor Flag.

*** This station was known as Whitney-on-the-Wye until 14 July 1924. It was first closed on 12 December 1961, and reopened on 15 January 1962 only to finally close just over a fortnight later.

**** Known as Hay until 13 June 1955. While most of the town is in Brecknockshire, the station lay in Herefordshire.

The Hereford, Hay & Brecon Railway obtained its Act in August 1859. Initial hopes for the line were high, with talk of it being extended to Milford Haven and providing a through route to the Midlands. The reality was somewhat different and the line had problems with its first contractor, McCormick & Holmes, who were replaced by Thomas Savin. The company also had an argument with the Oxford, Worcester & Wolverhampton and Worcester & Hereford railways which had both intended to work the line. As a result of this, a new Act in 1860 authorised a junction with the Newport, Abergavenny & Hereford Railway at Hereford Barton. The Hereford, Hay & Brecon bought the older, horse-worked, Hay Railway and parts of its trackbed were used for construction of the HH&B while other parts were used by the Mid-Wales Railway and the Brecon & Merthyr Tydfil Junction Railway. At the same time it was decided not to build the HH&B beyond a junction with the Mid-Wales Railway near Three Cocks, but to gain access to Brecon by running powers over the Mid-Wales and the Brecon & Merthyr railways. The first section from Hereford to Moorhampton opened on 24 October 1862 and to Eardisley on 30 June 1863, using the HH&B's temporary station at Moorfields, Hereford. The service was extended to Hay in July 1864 and trains started running through to Brecon on 19 September that year. The Midland Railway, which had limited running powers over the GWR from Worcester to Hereford, wanted to extend its system into the Swansea area and so took over running the HH&BR in October 1869. The GWR did not welcome the entry of the Midland into the South Wales area and blocked the entry into Hereford Barton Station with a locomotive and wagon. Consequently, the Moorfields terminus was used until the dispute was resolved in April 1874.

Locomotive No. 2287 with the 4.05 p.m. service from Hereford to Brecon and Locomotive No. 2275 with the 4.15 p.m. service from Brecon to Hereford at Hay-on-Wye Station 13 September 1956.

In July 1877 Midland trains started running to Swansea, using Neath & Brecon tracks beyond Brecon. The Midland leased the HH&BR from 30 June 1874 and absorbed it in 1876. Through coaches from Birmingham New Street to Swansea were provided, but these were withdrawn at the end of 1916 (although Swansea to Hereford trains ran until the end of 1930). Subsequently, trains ran only between Hereford and Brecon. The Midland could only run these local services as its running powers over the GWR between Worcester and Hereford were for goods trains only. In 1910 there were four return passenger trains daily between Hereford and Brecon, with an extra on Wednesdays and Saturdays, but only two went through to Swansea and there was no Sunday service. Besides local goods traffic the line carried a considerable amount of through goods traffic with five or six trains a day running between Swansea and Birmingham and vice versa.

Hereford to Grange Court *

Passenger service withdrawn	2 November 1964	*Stations closed*	*Date*
Distance	22.6 miles (Grange Court to Hereford)	Fawley	2 November 1964
Company	Hereford, Ross & Gloucester Railway	Backney Halt	12 February 1962
		Ross-on-Wye **	2 November 1964
Stations closed	*Date*	Weston-under-Penyard Halt	2 November 1964
Holme Lacy	2 November 1964	Mitcheldean Road	2 November 1964
Ballingham	2 November 1964		

Fawley Station, looking towards Gloucester, 23 April 1958.

* The closed stations on this line that were in Gloucestershire were
Longhope, Blaisdon Halt and the short-lived station at Hopesbrook.

** This station was known as Ross until May 1933.

Ross-on-Wye Station, looking towards Hereford, 11 April 1955.

The Hereford, Ross & Gloucester Railway had its roots in the Monmouth & Hereford Railway, which was proposed by the GWR in 1845 but, despite spending £59,000, was not completed. The HR&G was incorporated in 1851 with GWR support to build a line from Grange Court, on the Gloucester & Dean Forest Railway, to a junction with the Shrewsbury & Hereford Railway in Hereford. The line was built to broad gauge and was always worked by the GWR. The section from Grange Court to Hopesbrook opened in July 1853 and it opened throughout on 1 June 1855. There were some heavy engineering works, including four viaducts over the Wye and four tunnels which totalled over a mile in length. The GWR absorbed the HR&G in July 1862.

Mitcheldean Road Station, *c.*1907.

The broad gauge had been found to be a considerable inconvenience where it met the narrow (now standard) gauge and both goods and passengers had to be transhipped. The broad gauge was gradually done away with and one of the first sections to be converted was the HR&G. The conversion was made in two sections either side of Ross. London horse-drawn buses were hired to substitute for the trains and a week was allowed for each section. In the event the line closed on 15 August 1869 and opened to narrow gauge trains five days later. Much was learned from the exercise about the preparations needed for future gauge conversions. The section south from Hereford to Rotherwas Junction, a distance of just over a mile, had already been converted to mixed gauge to accommodate LNWR trains travelling to the loop around to the Hereford–Abergavenny line. In 1910 there were seven daily return services with one on a Sunday. Besides being a useful diversionary route when the Severn Tunnel was closed, it carried Hereford expresses. In 1947 a passenger service was only provided on weekdays, but of the seven down trains five originated at Paddington.

Kington Branch *

Passenger service withdrawn   7 February 1955
Distance   13.4 miles (Leominster Junction to Kington)
Company   Leominster & Kington Railway

Stations closed	*Date*
Kington **	7 February 1955
Titley	7 February 1955
Marston Halt ***	7 February 1955
Pembridge	7 February 1955
Kingsland	7 February 1955

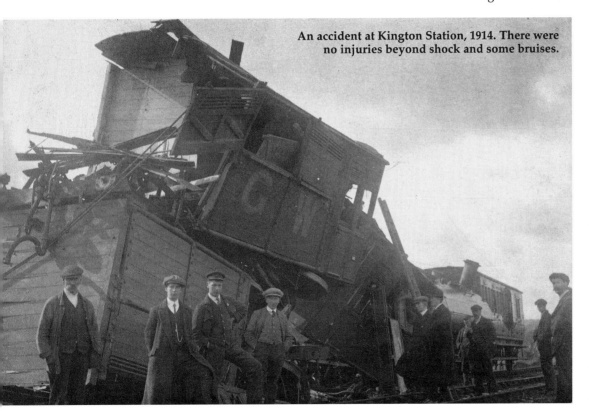

An accident at Kington Station, 1914. There were no injuries beyond shock and some bruises.

By the end of the eighteenth century, Kington was a thriving town and the roads linking it to the outside world were in a poor state due to the volume of heavy goods passing over them. An early attempt to improve the situation was the Leominster Canal which was intended to link Stourport and Kington via Leominster. This was not completed and in 1817 the tradesmen of Kington got together to build the Kington Railway. This line was built to the same gauge as the Hay Railway, 3 ft 6 in., which it joined at Eardisley before running through Kington to the lime works at Burlinjobb.

* In addition to the public stations, there was a private station at Oxhouse, between Pembridge and Kingsland, for the use of Lord Bateman. Closed stations on this line that were in Radnorshire were Stanner, Dolyhir and New Radnor.

** This station replaced an earlier one when the line to New Radnor was opened.
*** The earlier station here, Marston Lane, closed in January 1864. The halt opened on the same site on 26 April 1929.

Pembridge Station, 12 August 1932.

By the mid-1840s, the advantages to the town of being linked to the growing national railway system were apparent and there had been several proposals for a line through the district, linking Worcester and Aberystwyth. These proposals came to nought and instead many of the leading lights of the district had a meeting at Shobdon Court, the seat of Lord Bateman. An Act to build the line was passed in 1854 and Thomas Brassey was appointed as contractor to build the line and work it on completion. The decision to purchase enough land for a double-track line signalled a high degree of optimism. Construction proceeded slowly and the line opened for goods traffic to Pembridge in October 1855. By April 1856 the company was in financial difficulties and Brassey advanced it £10,000. The line formally opened on 27 July 1857, although public services did not begin until 20 August. Brassey's contract to work the line expired at the end of June 1862; he would probably have been relieved as he had complained in 1859 that he was losing £1,500 a year. The West Midland took over working and the GWR succeeded to it when it amalgamated with the WMR. The GWR absorbed the L&KR on 1 July 1898. The line was extended from Kington to New Radnor on 25 September 1875, having been built by the Kington & Eardisley Railway, which was worked by the GWR. In 1910 there were six trains a day, commencing at 5.30 a.m. from Leominster, of which only three went on to New Radnor. There was one return train as far as Kington on a Sunday. As this left Leominster at 5.30 a.m. and did not return from Kington until 7.45 p.m., the loco presumably returned light engine to Leominster. In 1922 the service was similar although the first train now left Leominster an hour later and there was no longer any Sunday service. In 1947 there were only five daily trains, of which only two went on to New Radnor. During the fuel crisis of the winter of 1950/51 the service was withdrawn between 5 February and 2 April 1951, and for the extension to New Radnor the closure became permanent. After withdrawal of passenger services, goods trains still ran for a while as far as Dolyhir.

Kington & Eardisley Railway

Passenger service withdrawn	1 July 1940	*Stations closed*	*Date*
Distance	6.9 miles (Titley to Eardisley Junction)	Lyonshall	1 July 1940
Company	Kington & Eardisley Railway	Almeley	1 July 1940

The Kington & Eardisley Railway came about as part of the natural development of railways. Its predecessor, the 3 ft 6 in. gauge, horse-worked, Kington Railway, had connected lime works at Burlinjobb with the Hay Railway at Eardisley. The Hay Railway became part of the Hereford Hay & Brecon Railway, a standard gauge line that used part of the Hay Railway's route. Although the Kington Railway had paid dividends as high as 3½ per cent it suffered severely from competition due to the newly opened Leominster & Kington Railway and, without its connection with the Hay Railway, the Kington Railway had lost its raison d'etre. The owners of the Kington Railway therefore decided that a standard gauge railway to join the new line was needed. An Act was passed in

Lyonshall Station, 13 August 1932.

June 1862 which enabled the K&ER to take over the Kington Railway. The original proposal was for a line from Kington to Eardisley with a branch from Lyonshall to the Leominster and Kington Railway west of Marston Lane. Later Acts provided for an extension to Presteign and a junction with the Leominster line at Titley. The line opened on 3 August 1874, being worked by the GWR. The further part of the Kington Railway, to the west of Kington, to Burlinjobb remained in being until replaced when the line to New Radnor was built. The Kington and Eardisley had been very expensive to build and had required seven Acts of Parliament (including the line to New Radnor). It was bought by the GWR on 1 July 1897; ordinary shareholders did very poorly, receiving only £2 for every £100 share. During the First World War the line was closed from 1 January 1917 and the rails were lifted for use elsewhere; it was reopened on 18 September 1922. The next war saw the line close again on 1 July 1940, but this time it was permanent. Services in 1910 were four daily return trains, reduced to only three by 1939. As usual there was no Sunday service. The branch train alternated its duties between the Eardisley line and the Presteign line and latterly was made up of an 0-4-2T, a bogie coach and a goods brake van. One wonders if the line may have influenced the makers of the Ealing classic *The Titfield Thunderbolt*: the train in that film was also a passenger coach and a goods brake van and could Titfield have had its origins in Titley?

Lines to Bromyard

		Stations closed	Date
Passenger service withdrawn	15 September 1952 (Leominster to Bromyard); 7 September 1964 (Bromyard to Worcester)	Leigh Court	7 September 1964
		Knightwick	7 September 1964
		Suckley	7 September 1964
Distance	23.8 miles (Leominster Junction [north of Bransford Road] to Bromyard Junction, Leominster)	Yearsett *	22 October 1877
		Bromyard	7 September 1964
Companies	Worcester, Bromyard & Leominster Railway; Leominster & Bromyard Railway; Great Western Railway	Rowden Mill	15 September 1952
		Fencote	15 September 1952
		Steens Bridge	15 September 1952
		Stoke Prior Halt	15 September 1952

Knightwick Station, 23 April 1958.

* This was a temporary station, used during construction and closed when the line was completed to Bromyard.

Locomotive No. 3725 at Suckley Station with the 5.50 p.m. service from Worcester to Bromyard, 17 July 1959.

To passengers travelling along this line in 1947, the last year of the GWR, this line would have seemed like a quiet branch crossing a very attractive, and very rural, part of the two counties. They would not have guessed the convoluted story of its construction, 37 years from its inception to opening throughout, and the three companies it took to achieve it.

Bromyard Station, *c.*1909.

The Worcester, Bromyard & Leominster Railway was promoted by local interests and the company obtained its Act on 1 August 1861, allowing five years for completion. There was considerable expense in purchasing the land and delay in letting the construction contract. Two years after construction began, in 1864, the first contractor went bankrupt and by 1867 the financial position of the WB&L was desperate. Before further finance had been obtained some of the company's assets were seized and sold. By 1869 the company realised it could not complete the line and applied to abandon the Bromyard to Leominster section. The line opened to Yearsett on 2 May 1874 after further finance was obtained. The remaining section to Bromyard opened on 22 October 1877 and was worked by the GWR, which absorbed the WB&L in August 1888.

Rowden Mill Station, looking towards Worcester, 11 September 1952.

The Leominster & Bromyard Railway received its Act in July 1874 following the abandonment of that section by the WB&L. However, construction of the first section to Steens Bridge did not begin until 1880 and although it was ready to open early in 1882 it did not actually open until 1 March 1884. The first discussions with the GWR to work the line were not successful and for the first few months it was worked by the Leominster & Kington Railway until the GWR took over working. The L&B was absorbed by the GWR in July 1888, that company having agreed to complete the line to Bromyard. It finally opened on 1 September 1897.

Fencote Station, c.1910.

The initial service from Worcester to Yearsett and, later, to Bromyard, consisted of four trains each way on weekdays only. There were four Leominster to Steens Bridge trains, worked in conjunction with the Leominster and Kington service. When the two sections joined, a through service of five passenger trains was provided on weekdays, trains running through to Worcester. There were two daily goods trains. The service remained largely unchanged through the years, although in the summer of 1923 a Sunday service was introduced between Bromyard and Worcester.

Steens Bridge Station, looking towards Worcester, 11 September 1952.

After its closure, the Leominster to Bromyard section was used to store about 600 unneeded coal wagons, many of which had been privately owned until nationalisation.

Stoke Prior Halt, 11 September 1952.

Lines to Tenbury Wells *

Passenger service withdrawn	31 July 1961 (Woofferton to Tenbury Wells); 1 August 1962 (Tenbury Wells to Bewdley)
Distance	5.1 miles (Woofferton to Tenbury Wells); 15.2 miles (Tenbury Wells to Bewdley)
Company	Tenbury Railway; Tenbury & Bewdley Railway

Stations closed	Date
Easton Court **	31 July 1961
Newnham Bridge ***	1 August 1962
Wyre Forest	1 August 1962

* The closed stations on this line that were in Shropshire were Cleobury Mortimer, Nene Sollars and Tenbury Wells.

** This station was sometimes known as Easton Court for Little Hereford.
*** This station was known as Newnham until May 1873.

From a map of northern Worcestershire the line from Woofferton to Bewdley looks like another cross-country branch, but its early history is more interesting. Tenbury got its railway in two stages: the first section was built by the Tenbury Railway from a junction with the Shrewsbury & Hereford Railway at Woofferton, using part of the Kington, Leominster & Stourport Canal (which had never been completed). The company obtained its Act in 1859 and the S&H supplied much of the land, it being surplus after the company had bought the canal in 1858 and drained it the following year. It opened on 1 August 1861 and was worked by the S&H (itself worked by the contractor who had built it, Thomas Brassey) from its opening. In 1869 it became a joint line of

Wyre Forest Station, 27 July 1957.

the GWR and LNWR, those companies having jointly acquired the S&H and it continued as a joint line after the Grouping, the LMS having taken over the LNWR interest. The section from Tenbury to Bewdley was built by the Tenbury & Bewdley Railway which obtained its Act in July 1860. It opened on 13 August 1864, but was worked by the West Midland Railway and later by the GWR when the companies amalgamated. It was absorbed into the GWR in July 1869. In March 1901, Cleobury Mortimer became the junction for the line to Ditton Priors. Services had an unusual pattern because, besides through trains which originated in Kidderminster, there were also a number of services from Woofferton to Tenbury. In 1922 there were five return daily through trains with an additional five from Tenbury to Woofferton and six in the return direction. Thus, if Easton Court was your local station you could choose from ten up trains (i.e. towards Woofferton) but not, of course, on a Sunday! The motive power in the early 1960s consisted of GWR tanks, ranging from autotrains worked by 14xx class locos, through pannier tanks to large Prairie tanks of the 61xx class.

Midland to Malvern *

Passenger service withdrawn	14 August 1961	*Stations closed*	*Date*
	(Ashchurch to Upton-on-Severn);	Ripple	14 August 1961
	1 December 1952 (Upton-on-Severn to Great Malvern)	Upton-on-Severn **	14 August 1961
Distance	14 miles (Ashchurch to Great Malvern)	Malvern Hanley Road ***	1 December 1952
Company	Tewkesbury & Malvern Railway		

Ripple Station.

The Birmingham & Gloucester Railway had opened a branch to Tewkesbury from its main line at Ashchurch in July 1840. The Tewkesbury & Malvern Railway began life in May 1860, but before it opened it got into financial difficulties and the Midland subscribed further capital. The line opened between Great Malvern and Malvern Wells on 1 July 1862 and through its entire length on 16 May 1864.

* The closed station on this line that was in Gloucestershire was Tewkesbury.

** This station was known as Upton until April 1889.
*** This station was known as Malvern Wells until 2 March 1951.

Upton-on-Severn Station, *c*.1909.

It was worked by the Midland, trains running through from Ashchurch to the GWR station at Great Malvern. The T&M went into receivership in 1866 and was absorbed by the Midland in January 1877. Although it was built as a single line, there must have been high hopes for the line as it was later doubled; possibly the Midland hoped to use it as part of a route through Hereford to Swansea. Despite this optimism, services appear to have been sparse: in 1910 there were only four trains daily between Great Malvern and Tewkesbury and this pattern continued at least until the Grouping. For most of the line's life there was no Sunday service, although in 1865, immediately after the line opened, a Sunday service of two trains each way was provided between Ashchurch and Great Malvern with fares of three shillings first class, two shillings second class and one shilling and tuppence parliamentary class. Midland 0-4-4Ts ran the service for many years but 3F 0-6-0s could also be seen in the 1950s. Latterly the line came under the control of the Western Region and pannier tanks were used. Although the closure date is given as from 14 August, there was no Sunday service so the last train ran on 12 August.

Presteign Branch *

Passenger service withdrawn	4 June 1951	*Stations closed*	*Date*
Distance	5.7 miles (Titley to Presteign)	Forge Crossing Halt	5 February 1951
Company	Leominster & Kington Railway		

*The closed station on this line that was in Radnorshire was Presteign.

The Kington & Eardisley Railway obtained powers to build a line to Presteign in 1864. When it did not proceed with the line the Leominster & Kington obtained powers in 1871 for a line from Titley. Construction was not without its difficulties: the bridge over the River Arrow collapsed and when the line was inspected Colonel Hutchinson commented that the bridges appeared to have been made stronger than needed. The line opened on 9 September 1875. Services were worked by the GWR from the start and an immediate effect of the line was a drop in the price of coal in Presteign by 5 shillings a ton. At first there were no intermediate stops; Forge Crossing Halt opened on 9 March 1929. In 1910 the service consisted of four return daily workings from Kington with an extra early evening train on Wednesdays and Saturdays, but there was no Sunday service. By 1922 this had been reduced to only three daily trains with an extra on Wednesdays and by 1947 there were only two trains daily with an extra one on Saturdays. The end came with the fuel crisis of the early 1950s. The service was withdrawn on 5 February 1951 but it was not officially closed until 4 June 1951.

Ross & Monmouth Railway *

Passenger service withdrawn	5 January 1959
Distance	13.1 miles (Ross to Monmouth Troy)
Company	Ross & Monmouth Railway

Stations closed	*Date*
Walford Halt	5 January 1959
Kerne Bridge **	5 January 1959

Walford Halt, looking towards Ross-on-Wye, 10 July 1959.

* Closed stations on this line that were in Gloucestershire were Lydbrook Junction and Symond's Yat. Those in Monmouthshire were Hadnock Halt and Monmouth (May Hill).
** This station was sometimes known as Kerne Bridge for Goodrich Castle.

The Ross & Monmouth Railway obtained its Act in July 1865 and opened on 4 August 1873. It was always worked by the GWR, which also built the extension from Monmouth (May Hill) to Monmouth Troy that was opened on 1 May 1874. The local company was not absorbed by the GWR until 1922. Although it ran through delightful scenery, the line was not well used and the peaceful Wye Valley appears to have been undisturbed by trains on Sundays. In 1910 there were five return trains daily, with an extra from Monmouth to Ross on a Wednesday. Of these, four trains ran through to Pontypool Road, an extra 18 miles. In 1922 the service was similar, but by 1947 trains were running from Ross to Monmouth only, although connections on to Pontypool Road appeared good. Trains took about 35 minutes for the journey from Ross to Monmouth (Troy). In its early days the line was worked by GWR saddle tanks and later became the haunt of autotrains.

Severn Valley Railway *

Passenger service withdrawn	9 September 1963 (Bewdley to Shrewsbury); 5 January 1970 (Bewdley to Hartlebury)	*Stations closed*	*Date*
Distance	39.6 miles (Hartlebury to Shrewsbury Sutton Bridge Junction)	Stourport-on-Severn **	5 January 1970
		Burlish ***	5 January 1970
		Bewdley	5 January 1970
Company	Severn Valley Railway	Northwood Halt	9 September 1963
		Arley	9 September 1963

* The closed stations on this line that were in Shropshire were Highley, Hampton Loade, Eardington, Bridgnorth, Linley Halt, Coalport, Jackfield Halt, Ironbridge & Broseley, Buildwas, Cressage, Cound Halt and Berrington.
** Known as Stourport until October 1934.
*** Known as Burlish Halt until 6th May 1968.

Stourport Station, c.1922.

The Severn Valley Railway was authorised in 1853 but did not open until 1 February 1862, by which time it had been leased by the West Midland. It was absorbed by the GWR in 1872. In 1910 the weekday service north of Bewdley consisted of six through trains to Shrewsbury and five return, with a number of others to Bridgnorth only. There were no through trains on a Sunday but one ran as far as Bridgnorth and another as far as Highley. South of Bewdley the service was much more intense: not only were there the trains to Shrewsbury but also there was an intensive service from Stourport to Bewdley and on over the GWR branch to Kidderminster. When the Severn Valley closed a preservation group took over the section from Bewdley to Bridgnorth while the section from Bewdley to Hartlebury is partly open to the public as a footpath. It is probably far better known as a preserved line and its trains are almost certainly far better patronised now than in earlier times.

Stratford-upon-Avon to Cheltenham *

Passenger service withdrawn	25 March 1968	*Stations closed*	*Date*
Distance	30.6 miles (Stratford-upon-Avon	Weston-sub-Edge	7 March 1960
	to Cheltenham Malvern Road Junction)	Broadway **	7 March 1960
Company	Great Western Railway		

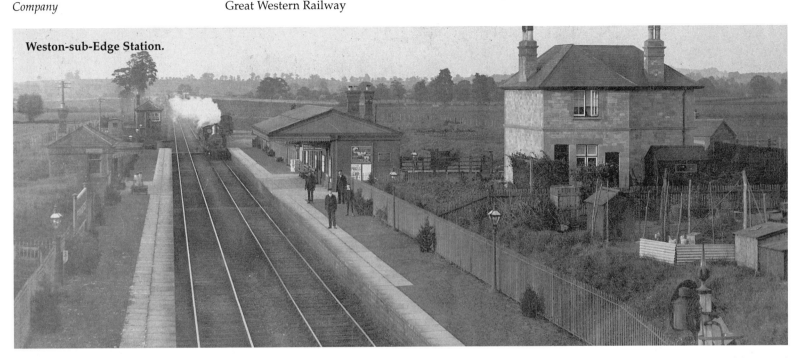

Weston-sub-Edge Station.

At the beginning of the twentieth century the GWR was in the process of reinventing itself. A start had already been made with the end of the Broad Gauge in 1892 and the new century saw new all-corridor expresses such as the Cornish Riviera (known as 'The Limited' because the train was of fixed length) hauled by modern locomotives, part of a new range of standard locomotives being built at Swindon. A major part of this new image was new lines removing some roundabout routes which had occurred as the railway system grew piecemeal in the previous century and which removed the slur that GWR stood for 'Great Way Round'!

* Closed stations on this line that were in Gloucestershire were Cheltenham Spa Malvern Road, Cheltenham High Street Halt, Cheltenham Racecourse, Bishop's Cleeve, Gotherington Halt, Gretton Halt, Winchcombe, Hayles Abbey Halt, Toddington, Laverton Halt, Willersey Halt, Broad Marston Halt, Pebworth Halt, Long Marston and Milcote. Closed stations in Warwickshire were Stratford-upon-Avon Racecourse Platform and Chambers Crossing Halt.

** This station was known as Broadway (Worcs) under British Railways.

Locomotive No. 9445 at Broadway Station with the 1.01 p.m. service from Honeybourne, 18 July 1959.

One of these new lines was the GWR's new route from Birmingham to Bristol. This involved the construction of a new line from Birmingham to Stratford, using the altered powers of the Birmingham, North Warwickshire & Stratford-upon-Avon Railway, which the GWR had taken over. South of Stratford the branch from Honeybourne was doubled and brought up to main-line standards, while at Honeybourne itself connections were made with the Oxford to Worcester line to allow running between Oxford and Stratford and between Cheltenham and Worcester. Between Honeybourne and Cheltenham a new line was required and the GWR obtained parliamentary powers for this in 1899. The line served a double purpose: not only did it facilitate the GWR's trains between Bristol and Birmingham, but it stopped the proposed expansion northwards to Birmingham of the plucky little Midland & South Western Junction Railway. Construction started in the winter of 1902/03. During construction the viaduct at Toddington collapsed, resulting in four deaths. The line was completed in sections from the north end, opening throughout on 1 August 1906. From Standish Junction to Yate, the GWR exercised its running powers over the Midland Railway, even though these powers had not been used since the Severn Tunnel opened in 1886. In 1910 there was a service of eight trains each way between Honeybourne and Cheltenham with two on Sundays. In addition to these local services a number of expresses used the route, including a new Wolverhampton to Penzance service (this service was only known as 'The Cornishman' from 1952). Although the line has closed, it is still possible to travel over part of it as the section from Toddington to Cheltenham Racecourse has been preserved and reopened by the Gloucester Warwickshire Railway, worthy successors to the initials GWR.

Closed passenger stations on lines still open to passengers

Line/service   **GWR: Hereford to Newport**

Stations closed	Date
Hereford Barton	2 January 1893
Tram Inn	9 June 1958
St Devereux	9 June 1958
Pontrilas	9 June 1958

Tram Inn Station, 23 April 1958.

St Devereux Station, looking towards Newport, 23 April 1958.

St DEVEREUX for KILPECK

Pontrilas Station, *c*.1909.
Note the Golden Valley line train in the bay.

GWR: Worcester to Hereford

Line/service		Stations closed	Date
		Newland Halt	5 April 1965
Stations closed	**Date**	Malvern Wells (GWR)	5 April 1965
Henwick	5 April 1965	Ashperton Halt *	5 April 1965
Boughton Halt	5 April 1965	Stoke Edith	5 April 1965
Rushwick Halt	5 April 1965	Withington	2 January 1961
Bransford Road	5 April 1965		

Bransford Road Station.

* This station was known as Ashperton until 2 November 1964.

Line/service		Stations closed	Date
	LNWR: Euston to Birmingham	Stechford Gates *	1 February 1882

* This station was replaced by Stechford to the west.

Line/service		Stations closed	Date
	Midland Railway: Birmingham West Suburban line	Lifford *	28 September 1885

*Replaced by another station of the same name on the Camp Hill line.

Line/service	**Midland Railway: Bristol to Birmingham**	Stations closed	Date
		Abbot's Wood Junction *	1 October 1855
Stations closed	*Date*	Norton	1 October 1855
Bredon	4 January 1965	Spetchley	1 October 1855
Eckington	4 January 1965	Bredicote	1 October 1855
Defford	4 January 1965	Oddingley	1 October 1855
Besford	1 September 1846	Dunhampstead	1 October 1855
Pirton	November 1844	Droitwich Road **	1 October 1855
Wadborough	4 January 1965		

Bredon Station.

* This station was known as Worcester Junction until 1 March 1852.

** This station was known as Droitwich until 10 February 1852.

Stations closed	Date
Dodderhill	5 March 1844
Stoke Works *	1 October 1855
Blackwell	18 April 1966
Top of Lickey Incline **	No date available

Stations closed	Date
Cofton Farm ***	17 December 1840
Longbridge ****	by 1922
Lifford	1 December 1844
Lifford *****	30 September 1940
Hazelwell	27 January 1941
King's Heath º	27 January 1941

Eckington Station, looking towards Worcester, 24 April 1958.

* This station was renamed from Stoke by 31 October 1840.
** No date is available for the closure.
*** There was also a station named Cofton; it is unclear if they are the same.

**** The earlier station of this name, a little to the south, closed in May 1849 and reopened on 8 May 1878.
***** This was the second Midland station of that name; it replaced that on the Selly Oak line.
º This station was known as Moseley until 1 November 1867.

2-4-0 locomotive No. 167 at Defford Station, *c.*1908.

Class 4P 4-4-0 No. 41039 at Blackwell with the 4.35 p.m. service from Birmingham New Street to Gloucester, 4 May 1949.

Line/service	**Oxford, Worcester & Wolverhampton Railway**		

Stations closed	Date	Stations closed	Date
		Norton Halt *	3 January 1966
Littleton & Badsey	3 January 1966	Astwood Halt	25 September 1939
Fladbury	3 January 1966	Blackpole Halt **	c. 1949
Wyre Halt	3 January 1966	Fernhill Heath	5 April 1965
Stoulton	3 January 1966	Cutnall Green Halt	5 April 1965
		Stourbridge Junction ***	1 October 1901

Fladbury Station, c.1904.

* This station was known as Norton Junction until 7 September 1959.
** This station was used only for workmen's traffic.

*** This station was replaced by another of the same name 400 metres south.

Stoke Works Station.

Stations closed	Date	Stations closed	Date
		Ford Bridge	5 April 1954
Berrington & Eye	9 June 1958	Dinmore	9 June 1958
		Moreton-on-Lugg	9 June 1958

Ford Bridge Station.